THE EMPTY AIR

POETRY BY TONY CONNOR

With Love Somehow   1962
Lodgers   1965
Kon in Springtime   1968
In the Happy Valley   1971
The Memoirs of Uncle Harry   1974
New and Selected Poems   1982
Spirits of the Place   1986
Metamorphic Adventures   1996
Things Unsaid   2006

Tony Connor

The Empty Air

NEW POEMS
2006–2012

ANVIL PRESS POETRY

Published in 2013
by Anvil Press Poetry Ltd
Neptune House 70 Royal Hill London SE10 8RF
www.anvilpresspoetry.com

This book is published with financial assistance
from Arts Council England

Designed and set in Monotype Bembo by Anvil
Printed and bound in Great Britain
by Hobbs the Printers Ltd

ISBN 0 85646 453 9

A catalogue record for this book
is available from the British Library

Contents

Part One

Part One

Centurion

That space is a strange one,
in which, behind a Browning Gun –
the breach blocked by a skewed bullet –
I shrink away from what must be done,
disclaiming, un-naming the act,
as if to annul it.

I am and am not there,
watching a nig-nog's nightmare-
scene in another man's slumber
explode to blind the fixed stare
compelled by the cracked
cartridge jammed in the chamber.

Cribbed and confined
by a tank turret, or flung from mind
into memory's afterlife, I fumble
blue funk and the tool designed
to grip, pull, extract
the misfired round crumpled

right in front of my face,
where I crouch in self-disgrace –
coward mind and cowering body.
And now I lose the place,
space and power to enact
that shit-scared swaddy,

that tongue-tied lad of eighteen,
battened down in a machine
with a sullen army of occupation.
I doubt my presence there – the scene
wobbles away from fact
to lodge in imagination,

the space present and past,
cramped like the tank's turret, vast
like the mind remembering, making
way for a shrapnel blast,
but leaving the tale intact
for all the fractures and faking.

Marble Cover

I like to write in a book
plain and unruled, with not
a hint of aesthetic ambition –
no fine, designer format,
no sign of lofty purpose.
This school composition book
is suitably austere,
with multiplication tables
at the back, and at the front
boxes in which to note
Subject. Room. Instructor.
As in my earlier days,
when I could no more
write a poem than score
a goal for the First XI,
I like the book's reminder
of unknown things to come,
of everything unaccomplished,
while I frown at some subject
in a room with dusty windows
and one of my favourite instructors
scrawls cryptic symbols on a blackboard –
Miss Goldstone, Miss Hartley, Miss May.
Today, as I turn the page
to write on the backward ghost
and slant of my earlier words,
I thrill again to the paper –
precious, not to be wasted –
of that ill-equipped, wartime classroom,
and of my mother's warm kitchen

where, forgetful of subject, room
and instructor, I drew aeroplanes
obsessively, on ruled paper
for want of a proper sketch-pad,
while hours slipped by unnoticed
on dark winter evenings.
Now, late in my life,
far and free from school-
mistresses and my mother,
I wait for flying machines
to form, this time as poems
upon unruled, blank pages,
soaring invisibly above
subject, room and instructor.

The Enquiry

His answer wasn't clear
on who should take the blame,
he downed another beer,
she didn't like his game

on who should take the blame,
she thought he should come clean
giving the culprit's name,
and this she took to mean

she thought he should come clean
whatever was at stake,
whoever might have been
the author of the fake.

Whatever was at stake,
he rolled his eyes and head
as if he couldn't make
much sense of what she said.

He rolled his eyes and head
like someone in a trance,
she felt she'd been misled
into a deadly dance,

like someone in a trance
who can't escape her fate
by guile, by force, by chance,
by full sight of the bait.

Who can't escape her fate?
His answer wasn't clear,
she'd never get things straight.
He downed another beer.

The Old Marquesa

Her chauffeur was Rix, a retired jazzman
who lived in a cottage on the grounds
and drove a battered van
when he drove at all, which wasn't often.
As for her own sedan,
an electric-blue, '62 Cadillac,

it stood for months at a time
in the locked garage, as if out of bounds,
except when her niece – the mime,
pothead, Earth Muffin –
smoked herself sublime
and drove it barefoot, fast, to the town and back.

A Fortunate Fall

Missing a front tooth
knocked out in early youth,
a watchful, close-lipped smile
settled my waking style,
as if fear of disclosure
generated composure
sufficient to withstand
flattery, reprimand,
accusations, praise
and love's engulfing gaze.

That day I fell on my face
to win a schoolyard race
made me begin again,
marked, among marked men,
the charming Teacher's Pet
primed to become a poet.

A Tale

There is a knife at your throat.
You are raped again and again.
It is a grim thought.
But worse: along the street
nuzzles a gang of men.
There is a knife at your throat.
The narrative will not wait –
the thing starts to happen.
It is a grim thought.
"You cunt ass tit,"
no heart, no soul, no brain.
There is a knife at your throat,
and stink and thrust and sweat
and death-fear and pain.
It is a grim thought
you cannot hold. You float
beyond, where it began.
There is a knife at your throat.
It is a grim thought.

Divorce

"You caused her a lot of pain",
my daughter says to me sideways,
mildly accusatory
on the first fine day of spring.

A dead woman – her mother –
has sidled into small talk
of other people's troubles.
Old hurts threaten our ease.

My daughter sits in shade
out of the fierce sunlight,
a four-year-old on her knee,
her eyes on the distant hills.

She answers her child's question
about a tinkling cow-bell.
I watch a contrail climb
high in unblemished blue.

Like many an old man
I am stiff and slow and calm,
made wary by arthritis
as much as by memory's traps –

so I take some time to reply,
rubbing my bad knee
and ready for a scolding,
whatever I choose to say.

Reading at Midnight

A spasm before bed,
sneeze sneeze sneeze
over an open book,
racket to raise the dead,
such shut-eyed, jerked release
of energy from the quick, –
suddenly wide-awake.

Somebody wipes a tear
and smoothes the sprinkled page,
showing no fear of ghosts,
strange or familiar,
and eager to engage
again with fictional lusts,
love-famines and feasts.

But back comes sneeze sneeze sneeze,
bookmark flips to the floor,
body beyond control
in convulsive ecstasies
of wholehearted labour,
as if each sneeze were soul,
self and animal.

Then a lumpish yawn,
the book banged shut
and nothing of consequence,
not even another yawn;
no dead to cast doubt
on mind's numb balance,
clenching circumstance.

Kitchen and Street

I see myself down a deep perspective of years
flicking peas from pods in my mother's kitchen
and fidgety with a monumental hard-on
upright beneath the table. Peas rattle
into a chip-lipped white enamel bowl;
I pinch my dick in feeble remonstration,
as if it were a disobedient pet,
but it throbs back rebel-thoughts. My mother
is singing a song from *No, No, Nanette*
as she washes dishes. The lodger is deep
in *Great Trials of the Century*, tweaking his nose
at another Black-Cap sentence, across from me.

And now – in old age – I make a graceful exit,
my hard-on gone, my household chore complete.
I might be any aimless adolescent,
kicking a stick to nowhere on the street.

An Absence

Bedtime brings a skunk —
I picture him out there:
stripe and twitching snout,
bushy tail and bright eye.

I lurch to the door drunk,
the sickly, thick night air
tells me, without a doubt,
he's grubbing grass nearby.

As for the actual beast,
the beast I might turn to use
in simile or metaphor,

he's just a stench released
to mortify my muse
as I wobble at the door.

Free Saturday

We walked from Buda to Pest,
across the famous Chain Bridge
built by a Scots engineer
in the nineteenth century,
she on an urgent errand
to cadge bits of string from friends
(she was changing apartments),
I tagging along to learn
how, under late Communism,
the locals managed their lives.
Well, they gathered short pieces
of string to facilitate
packing (boxes being scarce),
they worked for little money
at boring jobs, they patched sheets,
used soap carefully and read
newly translated novels
at night in their living rooms-
cum-bedrooms – also poems
disliked by the government.
On Saturdays and Sundays
they flamboyantly ignored
the dull-eyed Soviet troops
being led in docile groups
through deserted museums,
and when they could afford to,
they sat under chandeliers
in mirrored coffeehouses
where gypsy orchestras played.

The young woman on the bridge
was one of these citizens
and part-time interpreter-
translator for a poet,
an innocent from the West,
who was helping move her books
on a day without duties,
literary or social.

Much later we sat tying string
to string to string on the floor
of her crummy apartment.
We drank wine, stacked books,
listened to jazz, drew knots tight,
and then, using her friend's van,
moved ourselves and library
into her new living space,
somewhere across the city –
nearer the famous Chain Bridge,
Franz Josef's Summer Palace,
and the sole ice-cream parlour
outside government control.
She gave me all these details
between anti-Communist rants,
more wine and silly laughter
as we made pesto pasta.
Then, to fuel house-warming,
we drank more wine, smoked some pot
and talked of our families
ramblingly and to slight purpose.

She fell silent, on the floor,
waking to ask what I knew

of that great Scots engineer
who built the bridge – Adam Clarke?
I shook my befuddled head
and she crawled over to me
to offer thanks for my help
(so she said), deep-kissing me
and fumbling at my fly-zip
before slumping back asleep.

End of a War

Burning coals on a shovel: the kitchen fire
carried through to the sitting room at night.
Settlings. Coughs. Comedy from the wireless set.
Nothing important said, in familiar words.

Outside, light-streaks on rainy cobbles.
A figure hurrying past. A dog bent
towards a secret odour on a wall.
This is a year slow-moving to the next.

The Nine O'Clock News. The doorbell's chime.
Some woman come to tell a sorry tale
and smoke with mother. Chilblains. Constipation.
The bedroom landing grooms its punctual ghost.

Autumn in Age and Youth

At this time of year
my first street was treacherous
with a slick of sodden, blackened leaves;

here, a world away,
surly men with muffled ears
disperse the garish carpet with loud machines.

Bored, they aim
their casual, hand-held cannons,
forcing the flurrying blur into neat heaps.

My mother would scold me:
"Watch your step, look where you're going,
or you'll end on your back with something broken!"

and even now,
grown old in New England, I tread carefully,
walking among the moulted, managed leaves.

A head full of dreams
made me vulnerable *then*
to all-around-me unseen everyday dangers;

in age, my mind
dwells in a plainer place,
a full-fledged present, there to be known.

Which isn't true –
such certainties disappear
as sight fades, legs fail, trust grows fretful.

I watch the blowers
and ponder that heedless boy
who slips and slides, but keeps himself upright

dreaming a boy's future —
no bifocals, no wonky knees,
no old man's maundering thoughts among swirling leaves.

In John B's Café

"Can I bum a drink? – my wife just left me.
I ain't got no money or nothin'" he said.
"I feel so lonesome. I got no place to stay."

A few drunks watching the Midnight Movie,
myself in-turned, with much unread.
"Can I bum a drink? – my wife just left me."

My head is full of people I know
too well. I want to forget. Instead,
"I feel so lonesome. I got no place to stay."

"Mister, you look like a friend – a guy
who's seen some trouble. They call me Fred.
Can I bum a drink? – my wife just left me."

A gunman shoots. *"I drove from Iowa*
here." A sharecropper is filled with lead.
"I feel so lonesome. I got no place to stay."

"Mind if I come home and talk with you?"
It is like a book, or the troubled dead.
"Can I bum a drink? – my wife just left me.
I feel so lonesome. I got no place to stay."

Car Crash

A house loud with keening women,
familiar family faces changed
to the generations moving through them,
fierce and unrecognized.

A daughter killed in a distant shire –
cold on a slab, smashed and tagged.
The violent end always foreseen
by these gossiping disapprovers,
now grief-transfigured as time and place
toyed with particularity:
inconsolable Goddesses one minute,
howling animals the next.

Men glum: smoking, thinking.
The dead girl's brother locked in his room,
embarrassed by female relatives.
He'd never liked his sister.

Clear Night in Oxfordshire

Gemini shifts above me down the lane
in curved or infinite space beyond the bushes,
the clumps of cattle, the tithe barn and the lone
poacher who shakes from palm his pipe's warm ashes.

With snares and stealth he does as his father did;
my thoughts are on the holocaust that's coming.
He damns in silence the whims of a rabbit god;
I meditate on The End, while loudly humming.

Each from *The Bell* has gone his separate way:
I with his friends long-dead in distant trenches;
and he – what does he take along of me,
as he stumbles half-drunk through wet grass with his hunches?

It hardly matters. "I've seen the bad times, son:
I told the late Squire straight, in his own study –
that's fifty-five year ago. I've always been
a radical, son, the rulers they be a bloody

leech on the poor!" His Guinness to his lips,
I've heard him out with deference to the stories
the locals know by heart. If there are shapes
that I might make, they'll pass him like the lorries

a mile away on the M4 – streaks of light
cleaving the night to unknown destinations
he gives no thought to, where he curses failing sight
making more dim ancient nocturnal stations.

Old Bob and I, taking appointed paths:
one to the desk, the other to the dingle.
Both warm with beer, and warming to the deaths
we journey towards, and can't afford to bungle.

Evening in Adolescence

Leaves squelching underfoot,
a smoky glow in the air.
Distances disappear
into suburban twilight.

My feet. Youth comes back,
fragments fall into place,
or something presumes repose
in fiction, a crafted fake.

I linger under a streetlight,
sullen, rained-on, vacant;
"loitering with intent"
for a policeman's idle wit.

Sixty-five years ago,
if I was ever there,
but now vested here,
staunch enough to be true –

loitering with intent
on purposes unknown:
love, art, children,
this poem, this instant.

Hotel de la Soledad

The stranger flirts, with a sort of abstract grace,
using her cane and mine as a limping pretext
to stop me and converse on the courtyard cobbles.
Seized by her vaunting beauty, I am vexed
and surprised to be a man of seventy-nine,
still ready to let my life turn on a chance –
if that's what this is. My gap-toothed smile a sign
of lifelong, optimistic, ignorance.

Three Births

You decided our first child would be born
in the home of a former girlfriend of mine,
on a wooded hill beyond the town.
The frantic driver leaned on his horn
and drove at breakneck speed all the way
when he saw you were about to give birth –
groaning, puffing, grinding your teeth –
on the back seat of his swaying taxi.

Our second child took you by surprise.
You ate a large, spaghetti dinner,
announced you were going into labour
and festooned me from shirt to shoes
with the vomited meal. I barely had time
to summon the midwife and lay you down
on a sofa-bed – and the job was done,
another son and born at home.

A big, black, midwife from Port of Spain
helped you with number three. She smiled
inviting us in to look at the child,
then hurried us from the bedroom again,
so that you both could "Finish it up".
I took a photograph an hour later –
here you are nursing our new daughter
and sipping Guinness from a cup.

Vigil

I sat and watched that lead-hued flesh-lump
in death-like sleep, bright mind finally shuttered:
my old friend, hooked to a morphine pump,
his last *Gauloise* smoked, his last joke uttered.

Ensor and Friends

for Anne Cluysenaar

Happy as dogs relieved of cans –
cacophony-trailing tails – these bones
are glad to be rid of flesh. They freeze,
but rather that than the hot pains
of human love.
                            The painter draws
a stove, they come to warm their knees,
their hands, their lengthy sexless clatter,
laughter jiggling their paint-held jaws
at life, at death – it does not much matter.

They laugh, as do their friends the husks
of skittish gods, disguised as masks,
are frequent visitors to dull Ostend,
the little man who never asks
more of them than they wish. His hands
play games that please them.
                            Tilting, his mind
sweeps Christ in carnival to Brussels,
and they are glad. Gaily they guide his hands:
the organ hoots beneath his slackening muscles.

A Visitation, 1941

I saw a girl in Tyson Street
with ragged frock and ill-shod feet
whose lovely face was dimly lit,
as if she'd never thought of it.

Her mother must have sent her out –
perhaps with a coin, or perhaps a clout –
to bring home eggs, or milk, or tea
from Mr. Gilmore's Grocery.

Sublime in ignorant perfection
she sprinted off in that direction,
while I observed in breathless awe
whatever it was I thought I saw.

That grubby girl – whose gypsy eyes
looked into mine without surprise,
then turned away remote and bored –
lodged in my heart to be adored

as something nameless, come and gone,
before I knew what was going on;
a never-to-be-repeated presence
carried through life like adolescence.

She must be stiff-limbed now, or dead.
Our young eyes meet, with nothing said;
she looks away, new-breasted, fleet,
and disappears down Tyson Street.

Four Little Poems

April Activity

My Iranian neighbour, Medhi,
muses upon the woodchuck
that's stripped every leaf from his peas.
"I planted them too early," he says,
"there is nothing else growing
for the little creature to eat."

At Night

Outside the kitchen window
something looms in the darkness,
like a large, shapeless ghost.
It is the dogwood, bare for months,
suddenly in blossom soon to be gone.

Lunch Time

The women laugh together in my kitchen –
two of them – telling tales of silly men.
I eat my sandwich, as the talk grows raucous,
impotent, now, to earn such scorn again.

Comfortable Cardigan

A glimpse of threadbare elbow
returned my mind from its cell –
from meditations of death
and dear friends gone before me.

I stretched to appraise both sleeves:
the room shone, large with sunlight
and studious with good time
for poem after poem.

Black Dress–Gloves

Wearing them, I might feel like a stranger –
that preening fool, their late owner,
or the exhibitionistic poet
I knew in my distant youth,
who thought himself so very sinister:
leather hands, moustache, dark glasses.

But clearing fall's twiggy detritus
from my yard's first, spring warmth,
and at ease in the labour,
I flex, with friendly bemusement,
their supple fingers, scarred and roughened
by the common tasks I've set them.

Only the slightest itch of affectation
dares these benign ruins to gesture
grandly at Fate, or me, or the birds
flocking around the feeder,
but the gloves keep their composure,
familiars to my bidding.

As if forgotten, that previous master
and, never known, the dead poet
who flaunted their suave cousins
in the face of hushed listeners!
Satisfied, we return to work,
partners in the mild sunlight.

Poet in the USA

Nobody reads your words.
Nobody listens when you utter them.

Everybody is waiting for the bulletins.

Everybody is watching the bombs fall
with wonderful precision
on the latest, distant enemy.

And now everybody is merging
into everybody else
and nobody,
for a Statement by the President.

Annual Visit

i.m. Jack Marriot

You always seemed to be waiting for something –
though not my arrival once a year,
back at your door from the USA.

Yet the air of depressed expectancy
moving you glumly from room to room,
to show me your latest knick-knacks
and reproductions of 'famous paintings',
threw me into a subdued panic
of appreciative civility,
as if to mask a staring suspicion
that my yearly presence provided comfort –
like your dirt-dark house, the slimy soap
you never drained dry, the wireless
with no clear signal right across the dial,
the broken latch on the back door,
fiddled with but never fixed.

Or perhaps my visits were part of it:
the knowledge that everything *will* go wrong,
if only you've patience enough to wait –
for the cat to die, your knee to give way,
children to bugger off abroad,
and a wife to turn her back on marriage.
After that it was like a bonus
when the pub stopped serving your favourite brew
and a treacherous, erstwhile friend returned
wearing his New World smile of betrayal.

This sounds like a list *you* might have made
on one of your bad days, alone
with the few thoughts you were willing to think,
in a kitchen full of empty cartons –
where somebody found you four-days dead,
slumped in a threadbare easy chair,

on a date I haven't tried to remember.

Child in Chipshop

Under the maudlin strokes of a maimed hand
your small face smiles, though turned aside.
You look at me, to understand,
holding inquisitiveness and pride
in a nice balance, not losing your place
in the queue, despite that drunkard's stump of a finger.

Then order your "chips and peas" with grace –
remembering to add "with salt and vinegar".

Late Game

We played past dark in Boggart Hole Clough,
ignoring the strollers bound for home
as the bell closed the park – our life
and luck in that make-or-break game
being all that mattered. A glimpsed pull
in the gloaming; a shadowy fielder's claim
to have caught the batsman out; a yell
from a phantom at the bowler's end;
the unseen umpire's shout of "No Ball!"
and "Wide!" Notional cricket: grand
in mind – in imaginary space –
bewildering to real eye and hand.
Yet on we played, as if our choice
were mental over physical –
cricket played in a dream-place.
Until an invisible, boundary-ball
thumped a soft stomach hard enough
to deliver all of us from our spell.

Bad Afternoon

after Khodasevich

Today you'll find no nourishment
for comforting theories, self-deceits –
just organ-grinders, beggars, tramps,
the usual rain falling in sheets.

Streetlamps glow dully in puddles,
a pre-evening boredom clogs
your thinking, and descends upon
a ridiculous number of grey dogs.

Some sniff one another with wrinkling snouts,
some sniff themselves, some bark, some howl;
others seem lost in solemn search,
prowling the sidewalk, jowl to jowl.

Others, again, cock legs to piss,
a few are hunkered down to shit;
whistling them home from high windows,
their fat, complacent owners sit.

Rained off, dogged through and whistled out! –
your life's a trudge through deadly streets.
A shutter slams – you jump. Your heart
moves in its place, to prove it beats.

To Anyuta

Look at this match-box, see the picture? –
a small three-masted ship, full-sail,
is speeding along, all billowy canvas,
unmoving in a tranquil gale.

There must be a crew manning the vessel,
there must be a cargo in the hold –
cinnamon, cumin, rum and raisins,
barrels and boxes manifold.

And on the bridge, of course, a captain –
bearded, hawkeyed, valiant – stands,
who's sailed the seven seas times seven,
round misty capes to unmapped lands.

And somewhere on board a tiny seaman,
a young man live with love and song,
sits on deck when the sky is starlit,
gazing at heaven all night long.

And I, on dry land, in the Lord's keeping,
secure from harm in His master-grip,
am like that tiny seaman, sailing
nowhere at all in that tiny ship,

who, even now, in an aft cabin,
fresh from a song, or revery,
is staring out through an open porthole
at me and you – at you and me.

Vacation Land

after Khodasevich

Freaks of every shape and size
waddle ashore from the lake's ooze.

Foul weather claims the water-glooms;
the banks are alive with croaks and frog-gleams.

Lights go out, like thoughts in heads.
Clumps of tangled worms climb onto roads.

In the murky distance-without-detail,
a fluff-clogged, worn-out gramophone needle

skips, then sticks in a damaged groove,
repeating, scratchily: "love, love, love".

The soggy world is lapped in peace
except for thumpings from the grass,

where lecherous couples – ardent, zealous –
hump under cover of large umbrellas,

watched by a cross-eyed, big-mouthed gnome,
who slithers among the bodies, enjoying the game.

Family Funeral

My cousins light their smaller fires
beside the crematorium.
Near Floral Tributes, new and old,
they smoke – appropriately glum.

The women weep, as women must,
features awry on every drag;
the men stand full of silent strength –
lapel and understanding hug.

They mourn "Our Sister Edna"; all
agree the service was a treat.
Not saying much, they save their words
for times a joke will benefit.

Perhaps in the funeral limousine;
certainly in the funeral pub
they'll be their bantering, ribald selves,
making the best of a bad job

(the last of a generation gone;
a lost holiday, docked pay)
and I'll be with them, there as here,
strangeness disguised by bonhomie.

My cousins know the drivers, know
the man in charge, in a top hat;
seeing his sign, they dimp their fags
and move off, ready to depart.

I follow, family face intent
on likeness to unlikely kin:
a mourner un-consumed by grief,
a stolid man among stolid men,

yet bright with thoughts of smaller fires,
of correspondences to find –
and secrets I've let Edna take
into her favoured "Great Beyond".

Night Piece

The sky cleared of clouds.
The moon full. A few stars shining
through the sodium lights' upward glow.

Beneath heavy, dripping trees
he walks the deserted streets,
pleased to be out at midnight,
late in his life, with most of the town asleep.

No big surprises. A rabbit runs from a bush.
Through an uncurtained window
he sees a girl reading a book –
leant on a table, hands in hair.

His thoughts are familiar, too,
moving, knowledgeable and impotent,
among wars and other human woes,
as he takes in easy stride
Mount Vernon Street's gentle slope,
where it curves towards the sports field.

At the crest, he stops and stoops
to pick up a small, shiny object.
He looks at it closely. It glints in the sodium light.
He looks at the moon, then pockets the object,
as if he had lost it at that very spot.

And now he walks on – out of my sight,
out of my understanding, out of my poem –
whistling into the darkness of the sports field.

Meeting and Missing

i.m. Ken Smith

It might have been you I saw
in the Apostolok Szálloda
on József Attila utca,
sitting among the local whores
and Arab arms dealers:
a man with the look of absence on his face,
seeking his own curled self in another place.

And what about that time
we arranged a secret meeting
at Zur Goldenen Kartoffel
in Bad Godesberg, or somewhere
else Bad in Germany?
I was of Baker Abel Oboe Roger,
you in the youthful blue of an up-stager.

If indeed that was you
and not some slippery you S. of A.,
as later among the guy talk
the high, boozy, rockin' talk,
driven for out-of-county –
a blur of big ambition and petty need,
to be written, published, hated, put to bed.

Back with your old mates
back where, perhaps, you belonged,
did I meet you in a pub –
Jack Smartarse and Joe Dickhead
glued to the TV,

while you and a smoky man with a face like mine
talked of death and the use of the semi-colon?

Then, if one of us wasted years
in the Enterprise Zone,
the other exercised hard
in the annexe of unease
until he completely forgot
what he was training for. That's how we poets –
oracular, banal, – finish up old sots.

Delete *old sots*.
Go straight to prison. Press *Enter*,
retain the crumpled scratchcard
as evidence for the Inland Revenue.
Now, print our pensioners' skill
amid a darkening garden's varied green:
construers of loss and gut-ache, love and knee-pain.

And now a different darkening
under hospital bright lights,
the words fast running out –
just a few good jokes left,
some over-the-glasses looks
and the lost, last chance at games we never played
in Leeds long ago and wherever it was Leeds led.

Cancel word-play. Substitute
Vijay Bharati, Homer Simpson,
the nurse with a big bottom.
Ignore all rhymes and metrical structures.
Delete previous emails,
frontiers, gypsies, Friars Road, the sweet
fragrance of shed-side blossom, friends. Delete.

Unknown Voice

Body feels ill at ease.
Moving about its particular place
it aches here and there, or suffers sharply
a pain arriving from nowhere
in a chronically troublesome part.

Meanwhile mind in dull converse
with immediate supplicants
hears the distant uproar of an approaching mob,
entirely human in its desire
to wreak vengeance on its persecutors.

Between body and mind,
insinuating and mediating,
an unknown voice murmurs of possible peace –
as if a night sky cleared of hurrying clouds
to show a full moon and myriads of stars.

Part Two

The Poet's Life

This, then, is the poet's life:
pestered by powerful women
who think he possesses strength,
God-like wisdom and earned fame,
he takes them to his bedroom
and at elaborate length
proves himself only human
by talking about his wife.

Who lies sleeping on the bed
like a cinema beauty,
or an enchanted Princess
awaiting her lover-Prince.
Here, he says, is an instance
in support of my thesis:
a good wife shows a haughty
disdain for the fool she wed.

He always says the same things —
(each woman makes one visit,
and they never compare notes) —
which he *would* say to his wife
were she to whimper, or cough,
or otherwise indicate
she didn't want to miss it —
perhaps by twisting her rings.

But she has been comatose
ever since he first met her,
and the women shake sad heads
as he expatiates on

how she will soon awaken
to bake him sweetmeats and breads:
they know their own kind better,
and each has her secret woes.

Success Story

A dying Gielgud had once looked up from the floor
and whispered "Get into the light, dear boy!"
to the young spear-bearer on stage for the first time,
line-less and feeling far from Roman;
advice the novice cherished ever more
firmly through his long years of employ
in minor roles, until he stumbled into the lime-
light as a postmodern Willie Loman.

Well, he didn't exactly stumble. While playing a guy
in a Mamet play, with a carefully coached accent
at the National, or was it the RSC,
a Hollywood scout on the lookout for new talent
decided he'd be great in HBO's new, big bucks
series, *Death of a Salesman Redux*.

Death at the Vicarage

All Hallows' Eve. Under a gibbous moon
the village folk lay dreaming in their beds.
At midnight some few awoke to the sound of a shot,
but fell straight back into dreams of love and death –
though not one dreamed of the tragedy of their vicar,
slumped in his favourite chair, a bullet lodged
deep in his grey and sermon-spinning head.

*Statements made by persons interviewed at the vicarage the
following morning by Chief Inspector Parker of Scotland Yard:*

Mrs. Jonquil Fastlake

I may as well tell you now: the vicar was head
of a secret cult, "The Bridesmaids of the Moon" –
that's why you found fifteen of our members lodged
at the vicarage; none of us in our beds,
of course, when you arrived. Appalled at the death
we had trooped downstairs. No, I didn't hear the shot.

Colonel "Jumbo" Crampton

Are you suggesting *I* fired the bloody shot? –
look here!...Oh damn, I'm a bear with a sore head –
up all night. Frankly, I think this death
is the work of one of these women. Sex-starved, moon-
mad, the lot! The vicar spent so much time in their beds,
the Committee was sick of all the complaints they lodged.

Miss Celia Clegg

Complaints? Oh, those he *didn't* visit lodged
the complaints! Poor dear, I knew his bolt was shot

when he stopped "fair shares". But, as we make our beds,
so must we lie in them. *I* live in my head,
in case you're wondering. There was a time I'd moon
over men, but in me sex found an early death.

Ms. M. E. Simmons

It was awful to watch the decline and death
of all his youthful ideals! The man who lodged
with my Aunt Griselle, at Oxford, aimed at the moon.
The lecherous swine he *became* deserved to be shot!
But, God! – I loved every hair on the monster's head,
even when helping him, drunk, into others' beds.

Timothy "Jacques" Smith (the vicar's caretaker)

I was throwing some tea-leaves over the peony beds
when I heard the bang. I sensed the Hand of Death
immediately – but then, I'm psychic. At the head
of *my* list of suspects is that young ploughman lodged
at "The Bell". The vicar and he were lovers. The upshot
is this *Crime Passionnel* under a gibbous moon.

Preliminary report submitted by Chief Inspector Parker.

The sudden, violent, death of the above-named vicar
was caused by a shot that lodged in his head.
Aphrodisiac-impregnated tea-leaves found in the
    flowerbeds
are being forwarded for analysis by Crown Pathologist
    Moon.

A Night Out

The fabulous poet stumbled in grand style
into his favourite bar – a lowly dump.
His singing robes went unremarked,
somebody yelled, "Hi, Teach!" and left it at that.

He had pondered long the Augustan Mode.
He needed a girl, or a drink, or both.
Why waste exalted utterance? he thought,
and ordered a beer in so many words.

At the end of the street the River of Rivers
rolled on, rolled on beyond the Freeway.
He knew where he was – he was sure of that,
and what he represented, in a literary sense.

The evening was helpful. His spirit danced
to the tunes from the jukebox. His mind refined
the maunderings of a drunken girl
to a statement never so well expressed.

It was jolly and solemn. There was his Muse –
not half believed in – and there was his mind
preening itself for making good
with the faithless bitch's suggestive mumblings.

But who was her boyfriend? He did not know.
He thought of making a scene, and wept
invisibly. Another young woman
asked him if his name was Augustus?

He had to admit it wasn't. He left.
Outside the wind caught his Singing Robes
and parachuted him home to bed.
His wife shifted suspiciously, but nothing was said.

A Reception

The Distinguished Visiting Writer conversed
at length with the Distinguished Writer in Residence,
while casting a distinguished eye
around the room for evidence
of any Distinguished Writer he might have missed.
Eventually, dubiously,
his distinguished eye settled on me.
"Shouldn't I know you?" he said.
I shook my head by way of reply.

Visit to an English Country Church

MAN

    Well, here we are! I think the walk's
    not a great price to pay for this...

WOMAN (*to herself*)

    My God, he talks and talks and talks! –
    I wish I'd taken heed of Bliss.

MAN

    Pity your girl-friend couldn't come –
    Ecstasy?...Joy? – you know the one –
    there's nothing like a Tudor tomb
    for brightening days without the sun.
    I mean, the *artistry*, the sense
    of *reverence* – oh, how to say! –
    look at these painted pediments...

WOMAN (*to herself*)

    We'll be in this damn church all day!
    I thought at *least* I'd get a lunch
    out of this outing. Never again
    will I walk miles to see a bunch
    of effigies, through pouring rain!
    Wasn't Bliss right – "He's purest *nerd*,"
    she said, "all wind and PhD."

MAN

    Look at this charming, sculptured bird
    standing beneath the knight's right knee –
    it's allegorical, of course,
    the beak, you notice, firmly shut,
    a motif taken from old Norse...

WOMAN (*aloud*)

  Ow!!!

MAN

      Eh?

WOMAN (*aloud*)

         You're standing on my foot!

MAN

  *Aw*fully sorry! —'you all right?

WOMAN (*aloud*)

  Oh yes. Apart from feeling peckish.

MAN

  Good. Come round here, into the light…
  See that? — a sort of Tudor fetish.
  My dissertation (now a book)
  Effigies and Symbolic Space
  takes quite a *piercing*, major look
  at fetishism of the face —
  you see my point?

WOMAN (*to herself*)

         Oh, what's the use! —
  may as well smile, and humour him.

MAN

  You do! Now turn to these choir-pews,
  the light, I fear, is somewhat dim,
  but if you bend — no, get right down —
  see: carved beneath the central pew
  is Christ depicted as a clown…

WOMAN (*aloud*)

  Uh-HUH…

MAN

        It demonstrates my view –
as justified in Chapter Three,
(the nub of fifteen years' research) –
that when…

WOMAN (*interrupting*)

        I'm dying for a pee –
is there a *"Ladies"* in this church?

MAN

Er, what?…er,…*Oh!* – I say, you know
I've never *needed* one before…

WOMAN (*aloud*)

Well, carry on talking. I'll just go
and look inside the vestry door…

MAN (*his voice growing fainter*)

This feature is unique in tombs
carved before fifteen-eighty-three;
there *are*, of course, the catacombs
in Castelandra, Sicily,
but nothing like this architrave…

WOMAN (*aloud, to herself*)

He doesn't even *need* me there!
Look at him standing in the nave,
lecturing to the empty air –
thank God I managed to escape!
The door's unlocked – well, that's good news;
still raining! – On with Bliss's cape!
Now, where's the pub, I need some booze.

Part Three

Changeable Afternoon

Shadow dulls the waiting page
and the hand poised above it,
easing my reclusive thoughts
out of their hiding places,
hesitantly, as voices
whose slow gibberish relates
only by ancient habit
to my understood language,
then sudden sun dazzles sight –
shine of the desktop, trapped gleam
tangled paperclips give back –
and eager for me to write,
perhaps to make a poem,
words beckon me to my knack.

Youth

In tuppenny cinemas
I was myself entirely,
bored in church eager in school,
loitering under gas lamps,
suffering secret night cramps,
smiling-kind, inward-cruel
I was myself entirely
among homely enigmas.

Lacking height breadth thickness,
yet everybody's likeness,
haunting the familiar,
uneasy as a stranger,
no sooner present than gone,
a not-to-be-known someone.

An Outburst

I was seven, almost eight.
I remember the lamplight
outside the window, and her
sable coat trimmed with leather.
It must have been a cold day –
the kitchen fire was banked high,
blazing. As for what she said
nothing remains in my head.

Those harsh words were not for me,
anyway – I doubt if I
could have understood them, then –
though I recognized the plain
folly of their utterance,
falling on a dead silence.

Ritual

How many times did I wait
in the cold, deserted street
to usher the New Year in
at my mother's house – a man
youthful and suitably dark,
impatient for the town clock
to chime, dock-sirens to wail
another chance for us all?

I lobbed prescribed offerings
through the front door's openings
year after year: a black cat,
salt, coal, and things I forget,
bringing luck and good fortune
for the tipsy guests within.

Marching through Paderborn

"Fare Thee Well, Enniskillen"
blared the regimental band
to the ruined German town,
while we swung along behind
the music – victorious
over National Service
and all the indignity
of youth in 1950.
Such was the band's grand purpose,
transforming us, unaware,
a glory in every head,
even when, back at our base,
we reverted to the lewd,
loud, graceless swaddies we were.

Shadowing

A girl used to follow me,
furtively – seldom in sight –
a glimpsed ghost far behind
in the streets of Manchester.
This happened during lunch hour,
when I was at a loose end
though inwardly primed to meet
my doom or high destiny.

I was twenty, and alone.
The girl worked in Statistics,
down the same drab corridor
as mine, but on the next floor.
Why she shadowed me for weeks,
I suppose she must have known.

Old Soldiers

I didn't know my granddads,
or which enemy speared one
and shot the other. Two wars,
fought for the British Empire,
returned them, bent, sickly, dour,
to family and neighbours,
but both men were dead and gone
before I learned my first words.

They were never talked about;
their wounds and wars I've made up
from familial silence
and my wilful ignorance,
content to let their lives slip
away in surmise and doubt.

Wounded Concealment

My mother suspected me
of unnatural vices –
modern art, masturbation,
and finding good excuses
for others' bad behaviour,
being chief among unnamed
objects of her veiled contempt
and outright hostility.
But somehow she'd brought me up
to slough off disapproval
from righteous women like her.
Strong in wounded concealment,
I had years in which to find
the man I meant to become.

Hero's Return

She was wearing a black dress
when we met at a party.
Her shoulders bare, her hair loose,
her laughter loud and reckless,
she surprised me with a kiss
at once cold and intimate,
before my mind could focus
on her swift recognition
of me as a "final fling".
Her soldier would soon be home;
she had captured a plaything
for sex in the interim,
to be used, indulged, enjoyed,
and then freed, with nothing owed.

Two Voices

"We made love on the carpet
beside a bright Christmas tree.
I picture the scene clearly
except for her face, flame-lit,
staring at mine in mute trust –
face familiar to me,
now a blank disk merely,
as anonymous as lust."

"He wrote poems. I found him
amusing. We went out
for a few months one winter
in the seventies. We were
never really intimate.
I can't remember his name."

Fraternity

Roars of midnight revelry –
blasting music, laughter, yells
of drunken, young excitement –
reach my under-blanket ears
before sleep conjures away
consciousness and cleanly kills
me off, with no worse intent
than death to tease a dreamer.

I awake to aching knees,
solitude and bright sunlight.
The day invites indulgence
of old age's long distress:
in a welcoming silence
I ease my game flesh upright.

At Seventy-Nine

"Aching into my eighties",
that's one way of putting it —
suitable for a poem,
if not the orthopaedist
who'd want specifics, a list
of symptoms: neck? back? which limb?
For my purpose, a sonnet
lacking body will suffice.

But enough flesh to confirm
the indignities of age,
in the heft and reluctance
of this once-sprightly presence,
now a painful, brute bondage
as it approaches its term.

Speeches at an Eightieth Birthday

If the dead could be summoned
to say what they thought of you,
they would be as reluctant
and evasive as in life.
No eloquence from a friend,
no measured words from a foe,
would counter your sense of faint
virtue, lacking solid proof.

But why expect of the dead
more than of the loud voices
in present praise and debate
of your accomplished manhood?
Fading under fine phrases,
you disappear in plain sight.

Nocturnal

Sleeplessly pondering death,
as night waited for first light
to divulge the world again
in its firm, dependable,
long familiarity,
I stared into a blackness
polite to my mortal thoughts,
but offering nothing back.
For the murdered millions,
unmarked and unmourned – nothing;
and nothing for my dear ones
comforted to their last breaths.

At which, sleep ushered old age
into a dream of childhood.

Affairs of the Day

I expected a motet,
but the radio blared out
the coarse voice of politics.
Someone endorsed a Wealth Tax,
someone blustered about Defence,
someone talked Good Common Sense
concerning the Deficit.
I'd soon had enough of it,
and pressed "Auxiliary"
to listen to my CD,
banished the Republic's ills
for Gesualdo's madrigals,
his timeless, sublime music –
that wife-killing lunatic.

Late Life

The tedium of old age.
With so many pleasures gone
hours wait emptily – forget
seducing wilful Beauty,
or hitting the winning run,
or indulging a wild urge
to party all through the night.
Forget dancing, fancy-free.

Read books, smile at grandchildren,
attend to small household chores,
walk to lose those extra pounds,
and ponder things that happen:
floods, fires, famines, earthquakes, wars,
the deaths of yet more dear friends.

Afternoon Caller

for Sallie Hayden

She talks of infirmities,
her troublesome, failing flesh —
an inexhaustible theme
while drinking a cup of tea
at my round kitchen table.
With full reciprocation
assured by my aching knee,
or wrist, or shoulder, or toe.

But we bore ourselves quickly,
and shift to treacherous ground
where ills of the mind and heart
fight bloody, occult battles
masquerading as the world
going about its business.

Blizzard

Wind gusts in cold darkness,
swirling its burden of snow
in dense, confusing eddies.
One moment, the beech tree looms,
branches white-ledged, at my door,
another, and it's a blur,
or not visible at all.
I stare out, thoughts shuddering.

But turning to a warm room,
the unshaken composure
of shelved books and furniture,
I find myself firm again
in age and infirmity,
mind and its sustaining doubts.

Dark Street Curving

Where does the difficulty lie? –
with thought, word, echo, pattern, form,
or what comes into being when
simulated poetry
settles on the page, lacking charm,
trustworthiness, or even tune
recognizably born of sense
struggling with inexperience?

The long day falls away. Evening
stretches and yawns into late night
silence: a chair, a lamp, a book,
and outside a dark street curving
wetly deserted, out of sight,
like another poet's mistake.

Near the End

A small hump in the duvet,
she lies there, dying. Her face,
as if rehearsing its skull,
gapes at me: the mirthless grin
of her coming skeleton.
She, who tested my mettle,
full-fleshed, bright-eyed, mischievous,
in her great-hearted heyday.

Now she doesn't wish to see
me, or anybody else,
just let it soon be over –
children, friends, husband, lover,
the uncontrollable cells
wasting her drug-dulled body.

Indian Hill

Blossom trees and burial.
Time of renewal and death.
A psalm is read, a prayer is said,
a dear friend returned to earth.

I stand in the spring drizzle,
awkwardly trying to mourn
for someone who brought me ease,
as often as she would tease.

Other discomforted souls
shift feet beneath umbrellas.
Silent, sombre animals
that seem to glimpse their ending –
extinction of everything –
in this burial's dark glass.

Trysts

In star-besprinkled moonlight
young lover and murderer
move towards destinations,
solitarily intent
on clandestine encounters,
their yearned-for consummations –
one: billet-doux in pocket,
one: dagger closely concealed.

Much the observer misses,
much eludes the making mind –
such as the lover's kisses,
the murderer's fatal thrust.

Black clouds drift across the moon.
Words dwindle towards silence.

Part Four

Approach and Withdrawal

This looks like the same blank page
I've been staring at for years,
always in the grave presence,
the oracular presence,
of a grand poem that nears
and clears out thought to engage
the emptiness of my mind,
only to withdraw again,
leaving a riddling silence
to shadow my persistence
in fostering this token –
a poem humbler in kind.

Morning and Evening

I was brooding on the dead –
wife, sister, father, mother,
old acquaintances, dear friends,
an enemy, a lover,
everyone from my childhood –
when a glass slipped from my hands

and shattered on the sink's side,
like a claim on immanence
personified and made plain,
or like a minor penance
imposed by some household god
for kitchen inattention.

Sharp shards menaced my bare feet;
stepping gingerly sideways,
breath stopped against sudden pain,
now I was all soles and eyes,
full-bodied in the sunlight-
flooded, vinyl-tiled kitchen.

So another day began
in my seventy-ninth year;
and so I wrote a poem –
a six-evening endeavour,
of dubious invention,
to give misgivings a home.

Don's Lament

Trembling, close to the flesh
of women – their thoughts remote
and unknowable to me –
I answered evasively
when they spoke of love, and wrote
poems for them to cherish

long after my departure,
clothed in confident selfhood,
to find my ignorant way
through another working day,
when I would be understood
as attentive and entire.

Fool that I was, to value
so cheaply beauty and bed,
my fears and their aftermath –
charms against that little death
spun from my eloquent head,
ballad, sonnet, ode, haiku.

Doubly foolish to invent
an upright self, a creature
contrived in despite of lust,
love, poetry and the rest, –
a loyal, time-serving bore,
trusted by the management.

In the Classroom and Out

She hobbled to the blackboard,
her rasping, upper-class voice
mouthing, slow word by slow word,
the poem about a rose
she squinted at and slow-scrawled
across the squeaky surface
where ghost-faint sums still grumbled.

I was eager to snigger,
like every other young lout
lolling in the chalky air.
"Miss" was daft *enough*, we thought,
with her bald spot and loud laugh,
this poem was the limit –
she was boring our pants off!

But my true thoughts stayed hidden
among evenings when Miss May
gave me work in her garden,
where she talked to me kindly
of poetry, art and books.
Then, as light faded, led me
indoors for coffee and cakes.

Juvenilia

In my mother's front parlour
hung a little oil painting,
its overbearing gilt frame
curlicued and opulent.

The subject of the picture
seemed to be a man fishing
in a placid lowland stream –
the details shadowy, faint

beneath discoloured varnish.
I could just make out a gate,
a field with sheep, trees, low sky,
brush-daubs of face and hand flesh,
and what looked like a top hat
crowning the man's bent body.

I disliked that rustic scene
or murky semblance painted
in another century
by some clumsy amateur.

But when the room became mine,
I left it there – dull, dark, dead,
to caution and oversee
my poet's trance and labour.

Newspaper Delivery

Mr. Mitchell, looking out
at the pride of his leisure –
the vegetable garden
falling away in neat steps
from an ornamental gate –
treated me to the blank stare
of his preoccupation
with First-Prize-winning parsnips.

Wreathed in a cloud of pipe-smoke
at the door of his toolshed
he was lost, I thought, in thoughts
of weather, manure, rabbits
and Black – the bastard who took
last year's "First" with imported
specimens luscious as fruits
(though none could prove he'd done it).

I'd heard Mr. Mitchell's rant
over and over again,
so I placed his *Evening News*
on a low wall, tiptoed back
to my sprawling, rusty mount
and pedalled off through the rain,
lost in verbal niceties
and lines I couldn't make work.

Cold Day in Connecticut

He paused to prod fragile ice
trapped in a tractor tyre's rut,
unthinking in aliveness
of the day, of the minute,
and mind slipped unknown shackles
to sixty-three years before
when he knelt close, poking holes
in a frozen lake's border,
part-thawed through an afternoon
of back-lit cloud-banks slung low
on that boy, almost a man,
loitering his lonely way
somewhere in a baffled dream,
a slow route from youth to age,
from lake, to rut, to no claim
on seldom-questioned knowledge.

Yet took the road home by rote,
blackthorn swinging high, his mind
dwelling, settled and sedate,
on clear thoughts of journey's end.

Going for a Haircut

i.m. Alfred Hubbard

"Remind me of when I died,"
the plumber said to his son,
shyly conversational
on their way to the barber's.
The old man was eighty-five,
still fixing blocked pipes and bursts
all over the Cheetham Hill
town planners had demolished.
By the time Arthur told me
the story, his dad *was* dead,
and I was left wondering
whether I'd contributed
to his senile puzzlement
by writing his Elegy
over thirty years ago.

My Own Company

Why am I not confused
by shifting thoughts in layers,
obscuring wars with keys
and lovers' parts with prayers,
and jokes misunderstood
with beer I mean to brew,
and chances long since lost
with poems made askew?
Why am I not confused
by thoughts that will not rest
from moving through themselves
to form a palimpsest?
The mind construes itself,
or I construe the mind
as world-locked, self-engaged –
and kind to its own kind.
Its motions are my own,
familiar as the face
whose stranger's shifty glance
I never fail to place.

Face to Face

The woodchuck that hibernates
beneath my neighbour's backstairs
is ambling around again
now warm April days are here.
He's a frequent visitor
to my side yard's stretch of lawn,
going about his affairs
like a beast of fixed habits,

always taking a long route
to my house from the neighbour's,
with frequent pauses to dine,
snout deep in new-growing grass.
Most days I watch his progress
through a kitchen window pane,
but today I crept outdoors
to the porch – and sudden fright

when he looked me in the eye,
from close by, twitching his snout
at my alien presence.
I stood there, stricken stupid,
as if trapped by a leopard.
He bent to grub up some ants,
turned his plump body about
and waddled slowly away.

Dream Dance

Insatiable demands
masquerading as loose bonds
troubled my adolescence
and soured me with suspicions
beside women whose sweet dreams
turned gracefully from love-claims,

whose sleepy glances at dawn
made light of the devotion
that found in each clitoris
a mother's paralysis –
flesh I kneaded to dull pain,
like a dutiful, doomed son.

Black truth bruited in old age
from the body's hermitage –
too late for that injured beast,
immobilized by incest
and used again and again
by one bedridden woman.

No. 1 in A Minor

Listening to a quartet
by Bartók, I thought midnight
a companionable hour,
late in my only life: warm
room, lamp-thrown shadows, music
(quizzical, familiar)
and a quick mind, wide-awake:
bulwarks against the world's harm.

Delusions of solitude,
soon to be rolled into bed
with my recalcitrant flesh
and scourged all night in bleak dreams
of torture, death, and contempt
for the small joys we cherish
as we loll, benign, unkempt,
in defenceless sitting rooms.

But sleep is often dreamless;
why must mind run on, to tease
pain from an unformed future,
doom for my kind — and for me,
choosing to start this poem,
enthralled by complex pleasure,
alone and safely at home,
intent on a new CD?

Bewildered, but undeterred
by motions of mind and word
barely within my control,
I come to rest in the room
where my voice failed months ago,
after only eight lines – fool
of smug thoughts – to muse: here, now,
chastened. Properly struck dumb.

Part Five

Account of a Possible Coup d'État

1

Writing about his love-life
to an inquisitive friend,
he described it as "defunct" –
albeit in the bathroom
two girls (each claiming his name)
were locked in mortal combat.

On his desk stood the picture
taken at Bhubaneswar.
He studied it for a while,
oblivious to the noise.
"What did I do with that coat?"
he thought. "Did I give it back,
or is it in some closet?
Why do I forget such things?"

2

Rumours: All mail is censored.
There will be no salt next year.
The King has had a face-lift.

"If the way through the landscape
presents problems, go back
to Square One and start again.
In all probability
you are being frustrated
by preconceived ideas
which prevent the true beauty
of the cardboard trees and grass

from manifesting itself.
Postpone all big decisions;
watch your health on Saturday."

More rumours: The dam has burst.
The price of zinc is falling.
Snow-flurries are expected
over the Adirondacks.

3

Obscene Reminiscences:
well-known names discredited;
accusations of libel
ending in five legal suits.

On a shiny table-top
a single rose – reflected
in detail, but so darkly! –
lies where the loved hand dropped it.
Implying indifference?
Contempt, unvoiced, unwritten?
Secret dislike of flowers?

In the large picture-window
of the now-deserted room
sunset is prettily framed –
a lingering spectacle
nobody comes to admire.

4

"Men who resemble Mozart
(the composer) are ordered
to report without delay
at the nearest army camp."

A few words from a full heart
are worth umpteen treatises
on The Human Condition –
or so his old mother
(the stupid bitch) used to say.
But the times were difficult:
she was suffering from piles,
the apple harvest had failed,
the top attic was flooded
and it was common knowledge
that the central government
was in the hands of madmen.

5

Diagnosis: Bronchitis.
Prognosis: Fiscal ruin.

Between the cup and the lip
something had gone very wrong.
Bad enough that the tea-leaves
had already been used once;
that the mouth was rather foul;
that the arm was stiff with age.
The piece of statuary
kept wriggling oddly about
as if from embarrassment

at the examination.
The doctor from Vienna
swallowed his mental capsule
and spoke definitively
through his false beard.
The audience clapped loudly.

6

The haunted pavilion
(some beliefs held in common
by all reasonable men).

Messages from distant stars
(not the full explanation
we had been led to expect).

A referee's suicide
(negligible successes
among the uncommitted).

7

"The building is new," he said,
"but the fittings are antiques.
During the Pachyderm War
they were evacuated
to the Vatican cellars,
where they remained in the care
of monks for the duration."

"What an inelegant lie!"
the colonel thought to himself.
He had been billeted there

during the Biped Campaign
and recognized the tables,
chairs, carpets and chandeliers
as so many trusted friends.

8

Civilized gestures of love
made by a father-figure
in a somewhat public place;
a meditation on time,
space, death and eternity
disguised as incompetence.
During the fiftieth set
a disturbance in the stands
distracted both the players –
hinting that the stock exchange
was not invulnerable
to the plots of embezzlers,
and that the forecast showers
might be just what novelists
and poets were waiting for.

9

Following an argument
about testicle status,
three old men were arrested
for indecent exposure,
and the café was issued
with an order forbidding
the sale of intoxicants
for sixteen years and a day.

Dr. Drew's opium dreams
attracted no attention
from the town authorities.
He was a discreet fellow
whose known eccentricity
was innocuous enough:
he composed symphonic works
no orchestra would perform.

10

ENTRIES IN SOMEONE'S JOURNAL

"I did not like the morning.
First the *proposal* arrived
in a maroon envelope
(how affected Arthur is!)
then it began to thunder.
By the time my bath was run
I felt very dejected –
and almost swore at Dolly,
who is so long-suffering.

The Controller's face twitches
when Evening Hymns are mentioned.
They say he was once a priest.

He brought me a diamond.
I distrust his intentions
and told him so in plain words.
He smiled his 'official' smile
and called me a 'silly girl'.
He abuses his power
and is not above torture,

so my informants tell me.
Why do I put up with him?

The west wall needs repairing.

A *Constable sky* at noon."

11

Their liquor was well-hidden
under a heap of old clothes
at the back of the cellar –
but by the time they came home
the lodger had drunk it all.
He was found in a stupor
near the rhododendron bush,
his face red, his fly open.
Later he claimed that the shock
of some news he'd just received
(his grandfather's sudden death)
had unbalanced his judgement.
"A letter came?", he was asked;
"Well, no, a telephone call,"
he said with a shifty look.

12

THE BOOK OF SYMPTOMS. PAGE 5.

Damn! There are interruptions
from all sides; how can I think?

Delighted to be alive,
the survivors laughed loudly

at the mighty explosions
that destroyed the fuselage.
When their wounds began to stink
they laughed no longer; they cried.
This was in the ungodly,
swampy regions where the Raj
never held sway. They all died
before reaching the New Fort.

The tale – told by a one-eyed
silversmith in the bazaar
and embellished in good sort
by his loud apprentices –
has gone up and down the land:

"A foot dropped off, then a hand."

Dung-smoke; new moon; evening star.

13

Behind a marble column,
near the tomb of the poet
nobody gave tuppence for
until death shut his sweet mouth,
two Dukes squabbled in whispers
right through the Bishop's sermon.
That day the rocket went up
in a fiery, slow-motion
ecstasy, and on the shore
the oil-puddles slurped and globbed
around the remaining gulls.

In the State Art Museum
motes of dust gleamed in sun-shafts
and the elevator broke.
At the Birth Control Clinic,
florid gynaecologists
synchronized their watches.

14

A Confidential Report on ten artists
suspected of anthropomorphic views

(excerpts from a bad copy made on a Xerox machine)

NIMROD wears blue underwear
when he gives flute recitals.

GEISHA is being menaced
by phantom debt-collectors.

PILL has been contacted twice
by youths who *[illegible]*

[Illegible] at her house
for flagellation and such.

JUDAS keeps his dental plates
under an old tea-cosy.

LEAK *[illegible]* to pay
for his grandmother's vices.

SPODE has a female "cousin"
he goes on hiking trips with.

ONE-EYE has produced nothing
since he had his cuffs repaired.

AMAZON treats her children
to staged readings every night.

CURRY *[illegible]* why?
He must be *[illegible]*

15

Setting aside the deceits
of buttons and armatures,
the unworthiness of dice
and all the petty demands
of pipe-stems, smells and ropes,
we drew faces on our hands,
raised them like a strange device
and divided into groups
for assaults on foreign lands.

16

Glib-tongued car-salesmen in suits
have taken vows of silence;
how strange those moving-mouthed mutes,
each dressed like a deposed prince!

Soon (somewhere else) an edict
is thrown in the waste-basket;
letters are written, stamps licked,
a sick cat left with the vet.

But who can requite the love
of a Metaphysician?
Huge arc-lights shine from above;
the lame starter fires his gun.

And now fifteen famous men,
tired of seeming impotent,
select a central pig-pen
to prove that Truth can't be bent.

In a brilliant sunset
seconds prepare a duel.
Poor folk get what they can get
while stockbrokers rush to sell.

The car-salesmen will disperse –
so a wild rumour has it –
if the High Court will reverse
judgement on "The Biter Bit".

Beside a Romanesque church
on a neglected isthmus
neophytes stagger and lurch.
The moon rises without fuss.

The metaphysician drinks
with the cat's worried owner,
in a café where high jinks
are bare-breasted beneath fur.

Dark night, and the restless town –
at last – is under curfew.
The masses are bedded down.
The lame starter claims his due.

17

Hairballs full of teeth
are elevated to stardom.

The dirt under fingernails
escapes and crawls away.

Government proclamations
expunge themselves immediately.

Large veins take new directions;
legs fall off in droves.

A foul odour becomes fashionable
among the literati.

Rocks and pebbles behave like eyes
searching for something wrong.

The paratroopers waltz in,
bearing their breasts on platters.

Some new and recent poetry from Anvil

NINA BOGIN
The Lost Hare

NORMAN CAMERON
*Collected Poems
and Selected Translations*
ED. WARREN HOPE AND JONATHAN BARKER

PETER DALE
Diffractions
NEW AND COLLECTED POEMS

MARTINA EVANS
Petrol

JENNIE FELDMAN
Swift

JAMES HARPUR
Angels and Harvesters

NICHOLAS KILMER
Petrarch: Songs and Sonnets

GABRIEL LEVIN
To These Dark Steps

DENNIS O'DRISCOLL
Dear Life

JACQUES RÉDA
The Mirabelle Pickers
TRANSLATED BY JENNIE FELDMAN

NACHOEM M WIJNBERG
Advance Payment
TRANSLATED BY DAVID COLMER

www.anvilpresspoetry.com